WHAT NEXT?

A Follow-Up Guide for

New Spirit-Baptized Believers

By Paul and Mary Birt
P. O. Box 165
Millheim, PA 16854

HARRISON HOUSE
P.O. Box 35035
Tulsa, Okla. 74135

Unless otherwise indicated, all Scripture quotations in this volume are from the *King James Version of the Bible.*

ISBN 0-89274-053-1
Printed in the United States of America
Copyright © 1977 by Paul and Mary Birt
All Rights Reserved

Table of Contents

	Page
CHAPTER 1 You Have Been Filled	5
CHAPTER 2 God's Word — The Bible	7
CHAPTER 3 Praise	9
CHAPTER 4 Prayer	11
CHAPTER 5 Speak the Word of God Boldly	14
CHAPTER 6 Sharing	17
CHAPTER 7 Love	18
CHAPTER 8 The Family	20
CHAPTER 9 Holiness	22
CHAPTER 10 Fellowship	23
CHAPTER 11 Being a Good Citizen	24
CHAPTER 12 Dealing with Satan	26
CHAPTER 13 The Gifts of the Holy Spirit	28
CHAPTER 14 That You May Know Him	30

Chapter 1
You Have Been Filled

"Blessed are they which do hunger and thirst after righteousness; for they shall be filled" (Matthew 5:6). They shall be filled! And you have been filled even unto overflowing; for you have been baptized by Jesus in the Holy Spirit. For some the baptism in the Holy Spirit has come like a gentle dove settling upon the shoulder. For others it has come like a mighty rushing wind. Whichever it has been for you, it is the beginning of a new and closer relationship with your Lord. You have come into a new dimension with God. Now more clearly you can see the things of God. From you flows more love for Jesus than you have ever experienced before. You will want to praise Him more as you grow in this new dimension. A new love for the Word of God will come to you for the Author has filled you with Himself. Your love for others will grow for the love of God is shed abroad in your heart by the Holy Spirit. It is a divine flow from God. You have received power to witness boldly of your Lord to others. You will never be the same. You are in union, even sweet communion with your Creator.

What is it now that God desires to do in and through us? Where do we go now from this place? We need to look at the plan God has for us, and it is for this that this book has been written. It is intended to get you started in the right direction.

Chapter 2
God's Word — The Bible

God, by His Holy Spirit, will teach you from His Word. The Holy Spirit is your educator. God's Word will now become alive to you as the Spirit interprets what He has written either through direct revelation or through Spirit-anointed teachers and pastors. Learn to speak God's promises boldly. Spend time each day in study, absorbing God's Word and allowing it to become a part of your thinking and speaking. Just as the physical body needs physical food, so the spiritual body needs spiritual food. God's Word is our spiritual food: "Study to shew thyself approved unto God, a workman that needeth not to be ashamed, rightly dividing the word of truth" (II Timothy 2:15).

We are to study, not just read a bit here and there. (Several study guides and helps are listed in the back of this book.) God's Word is alive. It is supernatural. It is more than just a book. It brings life and health, prosperity, and peace. It brings wholeness and cleansing. The Word of God must become a part of us so that we speak it, live it, feed upon it, and rest in it.

You need to hear God's Word taught in such a way that your faith will grow and you will mature spiritually. Find a Bible-believing church that is moving in the power of the Holy Spirit so that you may have fellowship with like-minded Christians. Bible studies and prayer groups of people who believe in the full gospel for today may be a great help to you.

There are a few simple principles you can follow in rightly dividing the Word of God. First, read the same passage of Scripture from a number of different translations to gain insight and clarity. Words change in meaning and shades of emphasis over the years. The same scripture is sometimes stated differently by other translations. Second, the use of a good Bible concordance is helpful in tracing the subject through the Bible and also to give word meanings. Third, read the verses before and after the one that has your attention. Then read the chapter to see how the verse or verses fit the large setting. Reading the chapters preceding and following the chapter containing your verse is also helpful to discover the intent of the writer.

Use the concordance or marginal notes in your Bible to find other Scriptures on the subject. Remember, the Bible does not contradict itself. If you find one or two Scriptures that seem to disagree with the others, then do more praying and searching to learn the unity of the subject. Then decide what they all teach on the subject.

It is important to remember ". . . that no prophecy of the Scripture is of any private interpretation" (II Peter 1:20). The Holy Spirit of God gave the Scriptures and is able to interpret them to you. Do not read into the Scripture what you want it to say. Find out what men of faith say about the Scripture and do not get off on some obscure interpretation. Be honest with the Scriptures.

God is a God who does not change. We are the ones who must do the changing if we are to grow up spiritually. No one wins an argument over the meaning of Scripture. It is good to admit we do not know it all. Be teachable. Be willing to learn. Approach the Scripture with the idea that you want the Holy Spirit to teach you through study and the ministry of teachers, pastors and evangelists who build your faith and trust in God.

Chapter 3
Praise

The Holy Spirit can now give you words to praise the Father freely. So many times we want to tell Him more than our English language will allow. As you speak and sing in tongues it is a time of refreshing:

> For with stammering lips and another tongue will he speak to this people. To whom he said, This is the rest wherewith ye may cause the weary to rest; and this is the refreshing: yet they would not hear (Isaiah 28:11-12).

It is a time of edification or building up spiritually: "He that speaketh in an unknown tongue edifieth himself . . ."(I Corinthians 14:4a).

It is a time of sweet communion with the Father. We are told by the Apostle Paul that he sang and prayed in tongues:

> What is it then? I will pray with the spirit, and I will pray with the understanding also: I will sing with the spirit, and I will sing with the understanding also (I Corinthians 14:15).

Many people today say that they feel that they do not need to speak in tongues. It is like any other gift that God gives: we do not have to use it; but if we do not use it, we are missing one of the dearest blessings of our Lord. He wants us to be able to worship Him in our spirits, our hearts communing with His heart. He has provided His way for us to do this.

Praise of our Lord takes other forms also. Psalm 34:2 says we can "boast in the Lord." Psalm 32:11 proclaims: "Shout for joy," while in Psalm 47:1 we are told to clap and shout unto God with a voice of triumph. Psalm 105:2

tells us to sing praise and also to talk praise. We can also lift hands, (Psalm 134:2) and even dance for the Lord (Psalm 150:4, 5), using cymbals and other instruments. The main idea is to praise the Lord.

God calls praise the fruit of our lips in Hebrews 13:15. We are urged to . . . "offer the sacrifice of praise to God continually . . . Let every thing that hath breath praise the Lord. Praise ye the Lord" (Psalm 150:6).

There is power in praise. Read II Chronicles 20:1-30. Here you can see how powerful praise is in a very difficult situation.

Chapter 4
Prayer

"What is it then? I will pray with the spirit, and I will pray with the understanding also" (I Corinthians 14:15a).

We are to pray in tongues and with understanding:

"Likewise the Spirit also helpeth our infirmities: for we know not what we should pray for as we ought: but the Spirit itself maketh intercession for us with groanings which cannot be uttered. And he that searcheth the hearts knoweth what is the mind of the Spirit, because he maketh intercession for the saints according to the will of God (Romans 8:26-27)."

Many times we are not sure how to pray for a person or a situation. It is at those times when we are to pray allowing the Holy Spirit to pray through us. Sometimes He will give us the English words to use. Sometimes we just pray in tongues knowing that the Holy Spirit who gives us the utterance is giving us the words to say what the Father needs to hear. Yes, it is supernatural. It is not something that you think up. It is one of the ways of God. Someday when Jesus comes, we will not need tongues to pray to the Father, but as for now this is a way that He has provided for us.

Prayer in the Spirit is powerful prayer. It is easy to understand why Satan would desire so greatly to cause confusion and antagonism against tongues. Do not listen to his lies. God has given you a language with which to love Him and with which to pray. Thank Him for it and use it.

It is good for us to pray that we will have the interpretation for what we have prayed: "Wherefore let him that speaketh in an unknown tongue pray that he may interpret" (I Corinthians 14:13).

Not always do we have to do this, but God has allowed us to have the interpretation.

Learn to speak freely in tongues. If your vocabulary is limited, ask the Father to increase it. When we are first baptized in the Holy Spirit, many of us have a few words and as we use those we will soon discover that there are more and more. Some people from other lands have told stories of how they have heard people who have just received the baptism in the Holy Spirit speaking words of praise to Jesus in the language of the listener's native land. Some who have just received the baptism, upon asking for the interpretation, discover the same thing. They have spoken words of praise to Jesus.

Learn to pray claiming the promises of the Scriptures. Search them out. Tell God you believe His Word and that you expect that you shall have what you ask for because it is a promise in His Word: "If ye abide in me, and my words abide in you, ye shall ask what ye will, and it shall be done unto you" (John 15:7).

God has shown us in His Word how to pray for healing, how to pray that financial difficulties will be met, how to pray for people to be saved, how to pray for any need. It is in His Word becoming a part of us that we will discover how to pray for various needs.

Some promises are immediate upon receiving salvation. In II Corinthians 5:17 you discover you are a new creature in Christ. Romans 8:17 says you are an heir of God and a joint heir with Jesus Christ. Matthew 28:20 gives us the assurance that He is with us always. Also I John 4:4 proclaims that the Greater One lives in you. Christ in you is greater than the devil. There are so many others. Look for them as you study. Make them yours.

All promises in God's Word are yours as His child. You will see them work for you in your life as you are obedient and grow in your loving relationship with the Father.

As you pray and claim the promises of God, remember God's timing is not the same as ours. Continue in faith, believing, and He will bring it to pass (Mark 11:24).

Just a word of caution to help you. Sometimes you may be with people who may not understand the need to pray in tongues. It is well to be mindful of those you are with and not cause them to resent what you are doing.

Chapter 5
Speak The Word of God Boldly

God gave us His promises that we might claim them and boldly say them. As we say His promises more and more, they become ours. When they finally are said with our spirit, we will know because we know that they are so. Let me give you an example of this. Philippians 4:19 says, "But my God shall supply all your need according to His riches in glory by Christ Jesus." Say it this way: My God shall supply all my need according to His riches in glory by Christ Jesus. Maybe at the beginning you may find this hard to believe. It is so, and as you say it, you will discover that one day it will become so real to you that you will never again doubt that God shall supply all your needs. "The Lord is my Shepherd; I shall not want." I shall not want. I shall not want. I shall not want. Hallelujah, I shall not want! As you say it boldly every day it will become a reality to you.

Choose as many promises as you desire and say them in words that apply to you. For instance: I am more than a conqueror through Jesus who loves me (taken from Romans 8:37). When you say it this way, it is personally yours and will eventually reach your spirit and you will know forever that it is so.

Listed below are promises that you can and should say boldly every day. Make it a habit to confess God's Word boldly:

Daily He loadeth me with His benefits.
                                        Psalm 68:18

By His stripes I am healed. He took my infirmities and bore my sicknesses.
            Matthew 8:17, Isaiah 53:5; I Peter 2:24

Jesus is the same yesterday, today, and forever.
                                    Hebrews 13:8

The Lord is my strength and my salvation; whom shall I fear.   Psalm 27:1

My help cometh from the Lord.
                                   Psalm 121:2

I am seated in heavenly places and I look down on Satan and his demons.
                                  Ephesians 2:6

I am a new creature in Christ: all things are become new.   II Corinthians 5:17

Greater is He that is in me than he that is in the world.   I John 4:4

I am the righteousness of God in Christ Jesus.
                              II Corinthians 5:21

All that I do shall prosper.   Psalm 1:3

If God be for me who can be against me.
                                    Romans 8:31

He is with me always even unto the end of the age.   Matthew 28:20

The Lord is my helper, and I will not fear what man shall do unto me.   Hebrews 13:6

He gives His angels charge over me.
                                   Psalm 91:11

No weapon formed against me shall prosper.
                                   Isaiah 54:17

Christ lives in me.   Galatians 2:20

God is my refuge and strength, a very present help in time of trouble.   Psalm 46:1

He only is my rock and my salvation. He is my defense; I shall not be greatly moved.
                                    Psalm 62:2

Say these to yourself out loud. Romans 10:17 says "so then faith cometh by hearing, and hearing by the Word of God." Say them to God; say them to angels; say them to Satan. Satan cannot stand against the Word of God. Find others and make them yours. As you say them faith will grow in you. Find out who you are in Christ Jesus. As you read the New Testament, Romans through Jude, write down and speak boldly who you are in Him.

Chapter 6
Sharing

The Holy Spirit was first given and is now given that we shall receive power to witness boldly for and about Jesus. The last thing Jesus told His disciples was that they should wait in Jerusalem for this power (Acts 1:4). These were already saved people for their names were written down in heaven (see Luke 10:17-20). The baptism in the Holy Spirit came after their salvation experience enabling them to witness with great power.

This same power to witness now can flow through you to others. The Holy Spirit can point out to whom we should witness and when we should witness. Then there are times when we should remain silent. He will put the words in our mouths to say as we yield our mouths to Him. To be an effective witness our job is to fill our spirits with God's Word so that when we open our mouths we will be able to share His Word and not just our own thoughts. It is God's Word that will win the people to Jesus. Our mouths and hearts need to be full of God's Word.

We can ask Him to point out to us to whom we should witness. Then we need to be willing to be used, not being forceful, in our own power, but gentle in the Spirit of the Lord. Of course, we always, in every situation, witness by our lives.

As we fellowship with each other, we witness by the love we show for each other: "By this shall all men know that ye are my disciples, if ye have love one to another" (John 13:35). How will people know you are saved? It is by your love for others. You can run here and there, speak and speak and speak; but if you do not love the brethren, it is in vain. Spend some time in study of I Corinthians 13. This chapter shows the importance of love.

Chapter 7
Love

"... The love of God is shed abroad in our hearts by the Holy Ghost which is given unto us" (Romans 5:5b).

God is love and His Holy Spirit dwells in you. Because of this, pure, creative love fills your heart and flows from you to others. The love of God can flow through you to others as you will allow it to flow. It is there. God's Word says it is. It fills your heart by the Holy Ghost.

Jesus gave this commandment to His disciples: "This is my commandment, That ye love one another, as I have loved you" (John 15:12).

He commanded it but gave us all of His love with which to love.

We are to unselfishly love others: "... Thou shalt love thy neighbour as thyself" (Matthew 22:39).

The song is sung: "They will know we are Christians by our love." How true this is for God's Word says: "By this shall all men know that ye are my disciples, if ye have love one to another" (John 13:35). It's there — all the love of God — waiting for you to give to others. Jesus said: "As the Father hath loved me, so have I loved you: continue ye in my love" (John 15:9).

When we are born again, our spirits are reborn, not our souls and bodies. Therefore, as we present our bodies, a living sacrifice unto God and renew our minds with His Word (Romans 12:1-2) we will change our attitudes toward love and expressions of love. As our Father begins to show us through His Word areas of unforgiveness, selfishness, pride and so forth; and as we stop doing these things, we will be able to open ourselves more for the out-flowing of God's love.

We must lay down the soulish "'I" life. We must learn to put others first and ourselves second. God is not going to do this for us. We do it ourselves. We have a choice every day what we will do. We can decide to be unforgiving or forgiving, resentful or understanding, selfish or kind, boastful or humble, envying or building others up, in love, provoking one another or promoting peace. We that are Christ's must put aside those attitudes that are not the fruit of the Spirit (Galatians 5:22-26). The Holy Spirit indwelling you from the moment of salvation can bring forth this good fruit — if we allow Him to do this.

Chapter 8
The Family

The baptism in the Holy Spirit allows for more of the love of God to flow through us to others. The best place to begin to see this love overflow is in the home. The things you did before in and about the home and with the family should be better than ever. Now the love of God is shed abroad in your heart by the Holy Ghost (Romans 5:5b), and you are empowered by the Holy Spirit to witness with great effect (Acts 1:8). There is no better place to start than in your home.

Of course witnessing does not mean cramming the message down the family's throats if they have not experienced what you have or forcefully preaching to them. Always in the home it is not just what you say but mostly what you do that witnesses to the family. Do they see Jesus in you? Is the fruit of the Spirit apparent in your life?

Paul says, "But the fruit of the Spirit is love, joy, peace, longsuffering, gentleness, goodness, faith, Meekness, temperance: against such there is no law" (Galatians 5:22-23).

The Holy Spirit will help you to be loving and kind even in difficult home situations. A little phrase worth remembering is: "Your home is your first mission field." There is where it all begins and never ends.

We are to walk in love (Ephesians 5:2), being tenderhearted and forgiving one another (Ephesians 4:32). We are to work together, always looking for the good in the other and being interested in making them successful. We are to be as interested in the welfare and well-being of the others as we are in ourselves (Matthew 22:39).

Maybe there are some things in you that God wants you to change. Perhaps there are some things you are doing that you need to stop. We should always do only those things helpful to keep us walking as God wants us to walk.

Our Father wants us to be a forgiving people. He forgives us when we forgive others. When you know that you have done wrong ask those that you have wronged to forgive you. When they have done wrong forgive them. Teach your children to ask forgiveness and to forgive. Study together these scriptures on forgiveness: Matthew 6:14-15, Matthew 18:21-22 and Mark 11:25-26.

So much could be said concerning the varied aspects of family life. We hope that you will study the Word of God and discover what God has to teach you concerning the family. The following is a partial list to get you started:

Deuteronomy 6:1-9 (Israel now refers to the born-again believers following New Testament teaching.)

Proverbs 22:6	Proverbs 13:24
Ephesians 6:1-4	Proverbs 19:18
Colossians 3	Proverbs 22:15
Titus 2:1-5	Ephesians 5:18-33
I Peter 2:21-3:12	

Chapter 9
Holiness

Our Father wants us to live pure, holy lives. The Word of God will show you how, and the Holy Spirit in you will help you do this. The fact that we have been baptized in the Holy Spirit does not mean that we have received instant holiness. We need to cleanse ourselves and present our bodies a living sacrifice to God. We must renew our minds through the reading and studying of the Word:

> "I beseech you therefore, brethren, by the mercies of God, that ye present your bodies a living sacrifice, holy, acceptable unto God, which is your reasonable service. And be not conformed to this world: but be ye transformed by the renewing of your mind, that ye may prove what is that good, and acceptable, and perfect, will of God. (Romans 12:1-2)."

God wants us to live pure and spotless lives before the world. He grieves deeply when we fail to obey His commands. His Word says we are to deny ourselves, take up our cross and follow Him. We are called to be a separated people, in the world but not of the world (John 17:16). We are separated for service. We are separated for womanhood and manhood, as an example for the world to see, speak of, and desire. The people of the world need to see a blood-bought life, holy and true to the One who shed His blood for it. They need to see people living as if they are part of the Kingdom of God. There are no second-class citizens in the Kingdom of God. All wear the robes of righteousness. All are to be as He (Jesus) was and walk as He walked. Dare we walk as He walked? There is but one choice in His plan: "He that saith he abideth in Him ought himself also so to walk, even as He walked" (I John 2:6).

Chapter 10
Fellowship

"And let us consider one another to provoke unto love and to good works: Not forsaking the assembling of ourselves together, as the manner of some is; but exhorting one another: and so much the more, as ye see the day approaching" (Hebrews 10:24-25).

All Christians need fellowship. They need to share in worship, praise, prayer, and study of God's Word together. We are the body of Jesus Christ. We are baptized into His body at conversion (see I Corinthians 12:12-27). Just as a human body remains together, so we too must learn to function together so that the most can be accomplished for the Lord.

It is not good to go from one group to another never staying in one place. Nor is it good to only stay home and listen to tapes and study alone. We need the fellowship of one another. Surely our Lord's statement, "By this shall all men know that ye are my disciples, if ye have love one to another" (John 13:35), cannot be fulfilled if we only worship alone.

Chapter 11
Being A Good Citizen

The Word of God tells us that we are "strangers and pilgrims on the earth" (Hebrews 11:13). This place is not our final home. Our home as children of God will be in heaven. While we are on the earth, though, we have certain responsibilities to our country and our fellow man.

The Gospel of Jesus Christ can be taught, preached, and propagated most effectively in an atmosphere of peace and freedom. We are to pursue peace and freedom: "If it be possible, as much as lieth in you, live peaceably with all men" (Romans 12:18).

When decisions are made in the federal or local governments (church government as well) we have the privilege of sharing our opinions with all who will listen. However, there are a few moral principles that should guide our comments.

First, in order to avoid judging one another, and to keep from becoming bitter or resentful against another person, we should speak out only on the issues involved. It is best that we confine our comments to the subjects under consideration or the issues of the moment. By not speaking against a person's character we avoid the sin of judging another person.

Second, we expect others to treat us with respect and honor. Likewise, we should be considerate of others. There will be people who hold opposite views from yours on some issues or doctrines. Find common grounds for friendship and do not worry about these points of difference.

Third, avoid heated arguments over any issue. No one wins an argument. Bitter feelings and broken friendships are often the result of insisting we are right in our opinions. Be kind. Generally, we can learn something from others, even though we disagree with them.

All citizens are to be subject to those officials over them as long as they do not violate principles of life set forth by the Word of God. God has ordained governments (read and study Romans 13:1-7). We are to pay our taxes, follow the laws of the land, and honor our civil leaders.

As God's people, we have the duty of praying for our leaders. We need to actively work to support Christian candidates for public office and continue supporting them and praying for them when they are elected. Daily we need to take authority over the rulers of darkness in our country and locality (Ephesians 6:12). We need to bind them in the name of Jesus (Matthew 18:18a). The devil will do his best to ruin our country and our leaders unless God's people use their authority against him.

Timothy (I Timothy 2:1-2) encourages us to pray for our president and all men and women that are in authority at all levels of government. God is expecting His people to be faithful in their prayers.

God moves on our behalf when we pray. If we do our part in praying and pulling down the strongholds of the devil, God will do His part in making our country strong and giving our leaders wisdom.

Chapter 12
Dealing With Satan

The Holy Spirit came in fullness on Jesus after His water baptism. Following this enduement of power Jesus was led by the Holy Spirit into the wilderness and encountered the temptation of Satan. Temptation will come to you also. Study Luke 4:1-14. Notice that Jesus overcame Satan's temptations with the Word of God. Each time He said, "It is written," and told Satan what God has said. This is what we must do also. We need to know God's Word so we can boldly say out loud in the face of temptation, "It is written."

Notice that the devil departed for a season. Satan wants to destroy your Spirit-filled walk with the Lord and he will try in many ways to stop you, side-track you, and get your eyes off of Jesus. We must realize that he was stripped of his power at Calvary. Jesus through His resurrection, ascension and seating at God's right hand has given us the authority to tell Satan what he can and cannot do. Upon reading Ephesians 1 and 2, we discover that when Jesus sat down at the right hand of God we were made to sit together with Him. All principalities, powers, might, and dominion are under His feet. Since we the Church are His body, of which He is the Head, all these demonic powers are also under our feet: "Submit yourselves therefore to God. Resist the devil, and he will flee from you" (James 4:7).

We are told to resist him. Of course we must be submitted to God first or Satan will just ignore us. Because of what Christ has done for us we can resist Satan in the Name of Jesus and with the Word of God.

As you look again at Luke 4:1-14, you will notice in verse 14 that Jesus returned from His wilderness experience "in the power of the Spirit." This is our example. We can be victorious over every temptation and come through in the power of the Spirit. Of course if you do not know what the Word says, it would be difficult to say, "It is written." The Scriptures in the Fifth Chapter, Speak the Word of God Boldly, will help you. There are many more. Find what fits the situation and make it yours.

The Name of Jesus has more power than any name. We can tell Satan in the Name of Jesus to leave us, and he must flee. Each morning after praising the Lord and praying it would be good to spend just a few seconds telling Satan what he can and cannot do that day. The following is a suggestion of how you might do this.

> Satan, in the Name of Jesus Christ, the Son of the living God whom I serve and to whom I belong, I bind you. For it is written: "Whatsoever ye shall bind on earth shall be bound in heaven" (Matthew 18:18a). Therefore, this day I bind you, Satan, and all your principalities, powers, rulers of darkness, all you evil angels and demons. I bind you in the lives of my family and myself. I bind you and forbid you to come against (list the people here for whom you are praying) this day. I cover us, them, and their property with the Blood of Jesus Christ so you cannot afflict them.
>
> The Greater One lives within me. I am an heir of God and a joint heir with Jesus Christ. My name is written down in the Lamb's Book of Life. Christ is my head and I belong to Him. You are defeated in my life. I have victory over you today for I am seated in heavenly places and you are beneath my feet. Hallelujah! Praise God!
>
> Heavenly Father, I thank you for the power and authority given to me as your child. Thank you for all Jesus has done for me. In His Name. Amen.

Chapter 13
The Gifts of the Holy Spirit

The ability of speaking in an unknown tongue which you received when you were baptized in the Holy Spirit is for the purpose of edifying yourself or building up yourself spiritually (I Corinthians 14:4a). Exercise that gift as often as possible each day. You can operate this personal gift any time you choose to do so.

The Holy Spirit has provided nine special gifts for the benefit of the body of believers which are listed in I Corinthians 12:8-10. These gifts or abilities operate in a person's life when the Holy Spirit desires to move in a worship service where God is being honored.

Additional gifts are listed in I Corinthians 12:28 and Ephesians 4:11. The purpose of the gifts is "for the equipping of the saints for the work of service, to the building up of the body of Christ; until we all attain to the unity of the faith, and of the knowledge of the Son of God, to a mature man, to the measure of the stature which belongs to the fulness of Christ" (Ephesians 4:12-13 New American Standard).

All gifts, abilities and powers which the Holy Spirit may operate through your life must be handled by you in love. The greatest gift a person can have is the gift of love. This gift governs all other gifts. The Holy Spirit operates in love through people: "Though I speak with the tongues of men and of angels, and have not charity (love), I am become as sounding brass, or a tinkling cymbal" (I Corinthians 13:1).

God has placed this chapter on love between two chapters which teach about spiritual gifts. We learn from this center chapter how to treat our brethren. We are not super-spiritual people because gifts operate in our lives. Neither do these gifts mean we are more mature than others around us. The baptism in the Holy Spirit and the privilege of being used by the Holy Spirit should make us more humble. We ought to be better servants of others than before our baptism: "Pride goeth before destruction, and a haughty spirit before a fall" (Proverbs 16:18).

This should be a warning to us to watch our attitudes. The love of God within you wants to govern every area of your life. The gifts operated in love are to bring unity, inspiration, and spiritual growth to you and those with whom you worship.

Chapter 14
That You May Know Him

Now it came to pass, as they went, that he entered into a certain village: and a certain woman named Martha received him into her house. And she had a sister called Mary, which also sat at Jesus' feet, and heard his word. But Martha was cumbered about much serving, and came to him, and said, Lord, dost thou not care that my sister hath left me to serve alone? Bid her therefore that she help me.

And Jesus answered and said unto her, Martha, Martha, thou are careful and troubled about many things: But one thing is needful: and Mary hath chosen that good part, which shall not be taken away from her" (Luke 10:38-42).

Jesus spoke to Martha and said that Mary had chosen the good part. Now He did not mean that you should not work. He was saying that sitting at His feet in worship of Him and listening to His words was the very best. It is easy not to find time for this very best. We need to spend time praying in tongues, reading and studying His Word, and waiting in quietness before Him. Allow Him to speak to your heart. Sing to Him, praise Him, and love Him. Our time alone with our Lord is prime time. It is the time that will equip us for service, empower us to witness boldly, and build us spiritually.

May you all say with the apostle Paul:

(For my determined purpose is) that I may know Him — that I may progressively become more deeply and intimately acquainted with Him, perceiving and recognizing and understanding (the wonders of His Person) more strongly and more clearly. And that I may in that same way come to know the power outflowing from His resurrection (which it exerts over believers); and that I may so share His sufferings as to be continually transformed (in spirit into His likeness even) to His death (Philippians 3:10 Amplified Bible).

Some study helps to get you started:

"Now That You've Been Baptized In the Holy Spirit" — Donald Gee

"Thresholds of Faith" — Kenneth E. Hagin

"Prevailing Prayer to Peace" — Kenneth E. Hagin

"Authority of the Believer" — Kenneth E. Hagin

"There's A Miracle In Your Mouth" — John Osteen

"An Expository Dictionary of New Testament Words" — W. E. Vine

"Strong's Exhaustive Concordance of the Bible" — James Strong

Other Material by Harrison House

It All Began in Slate Valley

Testimony by Henry Alloway — Pastor of St. Paul's United Methodist Church, Conroe, Texas   **$2.50**

The Eyes of Your Faith

Teaching on faith by Evangelist Ben Ferrell   **$1.00**

Words of Victory

Packet of 31 personalized scripture verses designed to make God's Word a reality in your life by Evangelist Billy Joe Daugherty, Magnolia, Ark.   **$1.50**